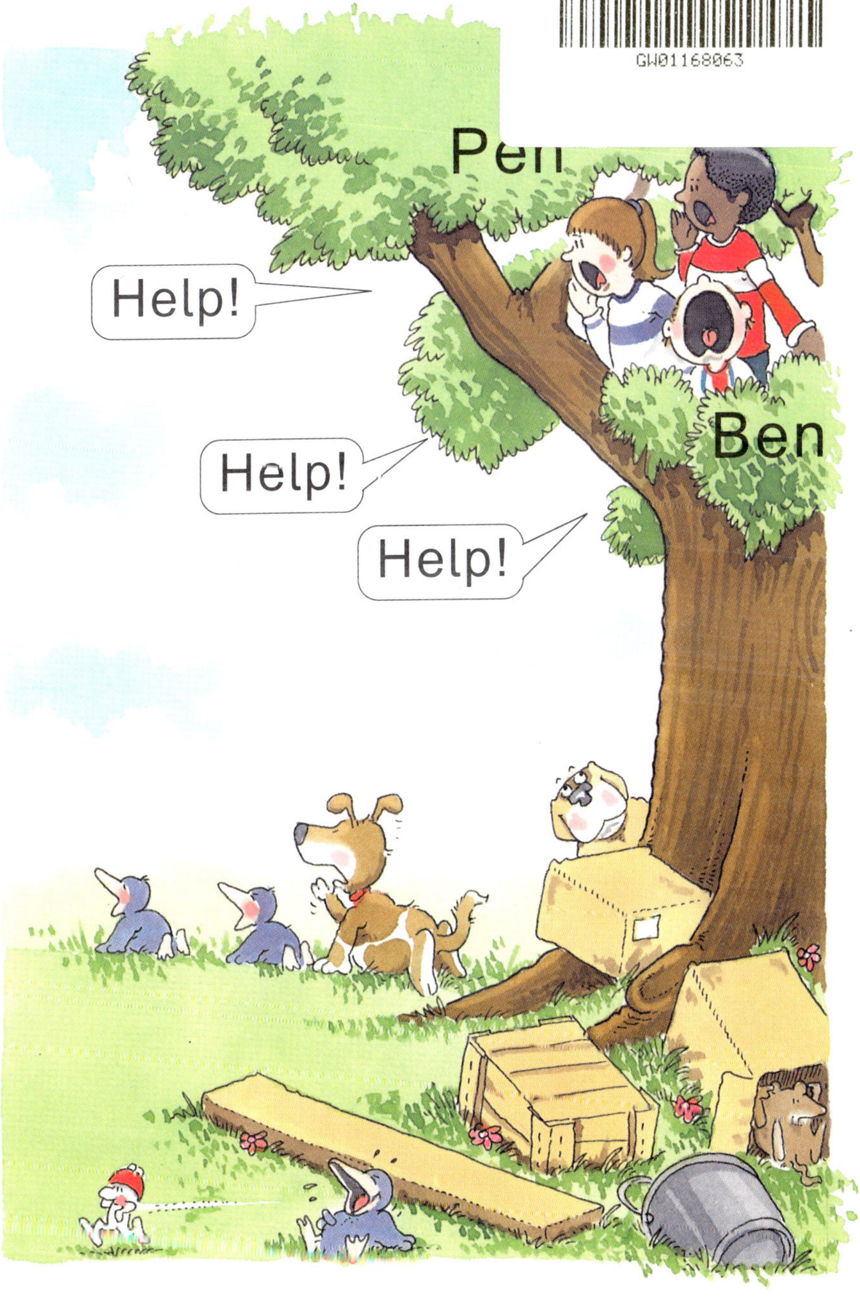
Pen
Help!
Help!
Help!
Ben

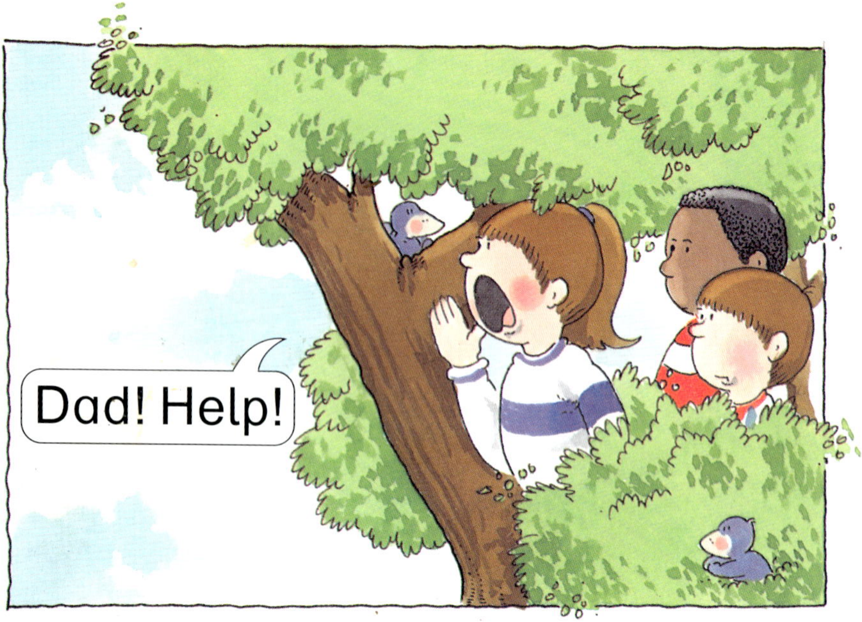

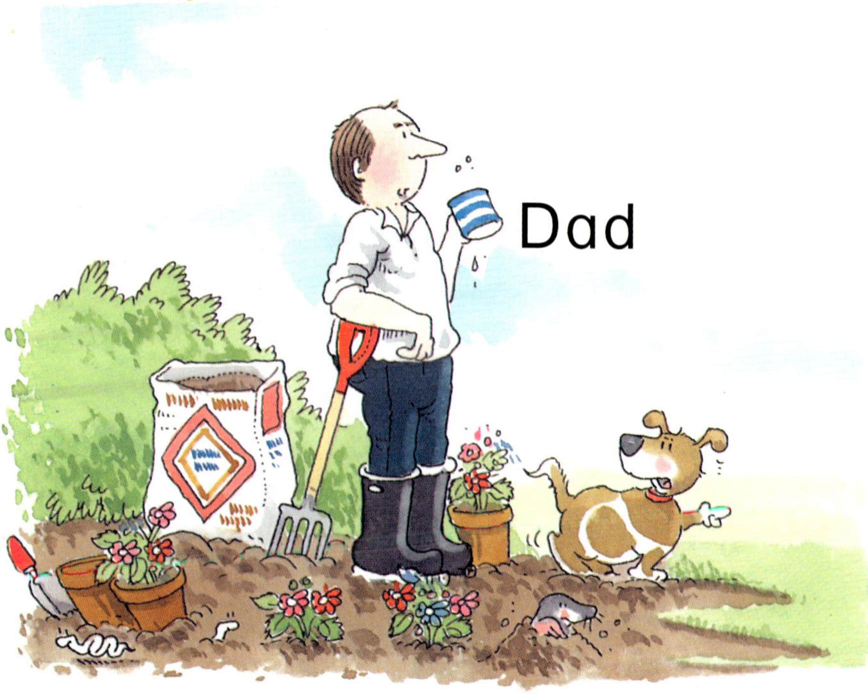

Dad

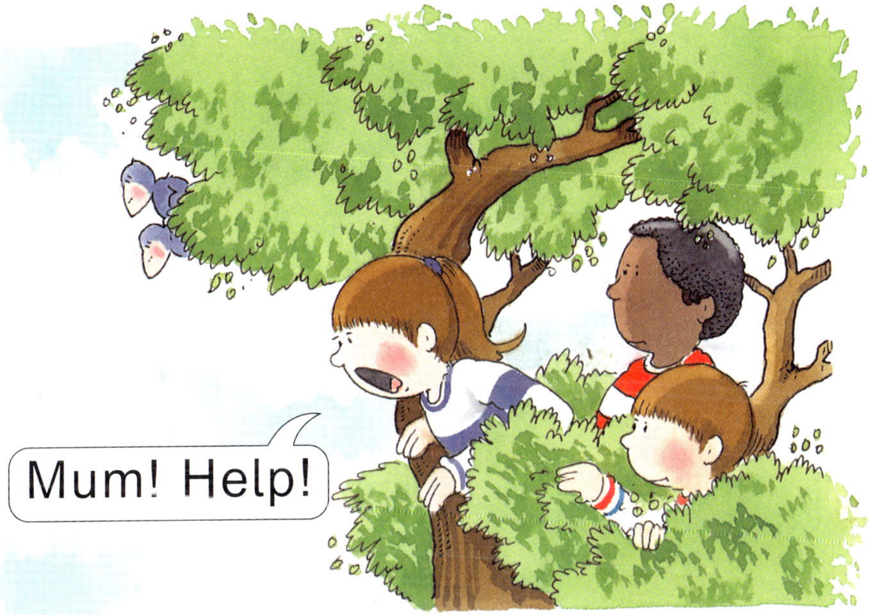
Mum! Help!

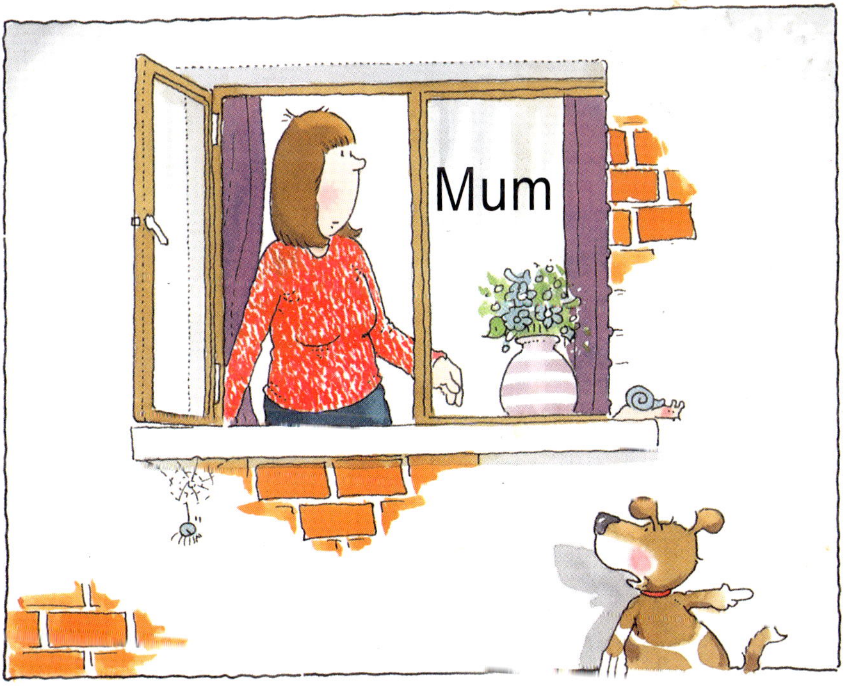
Mum

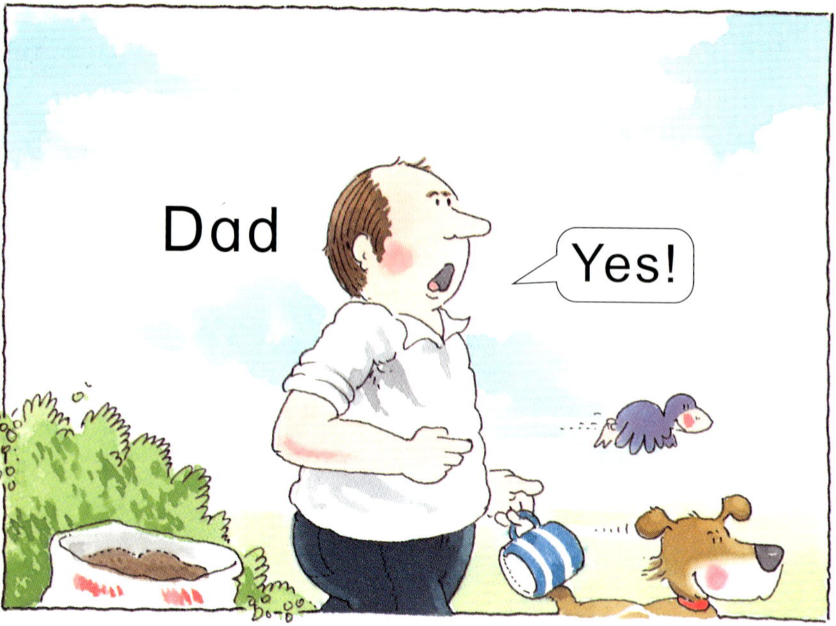
Dad
Yes!

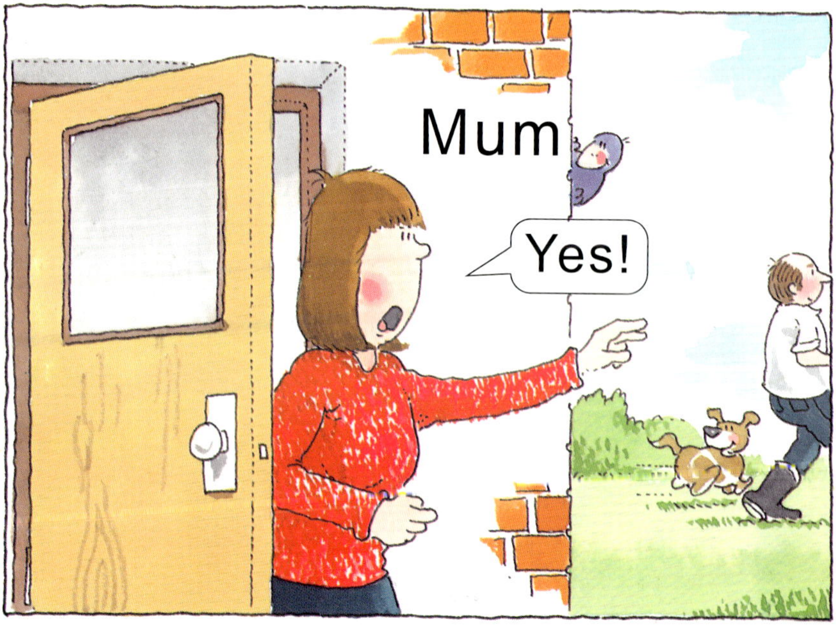
Mum
Yes!

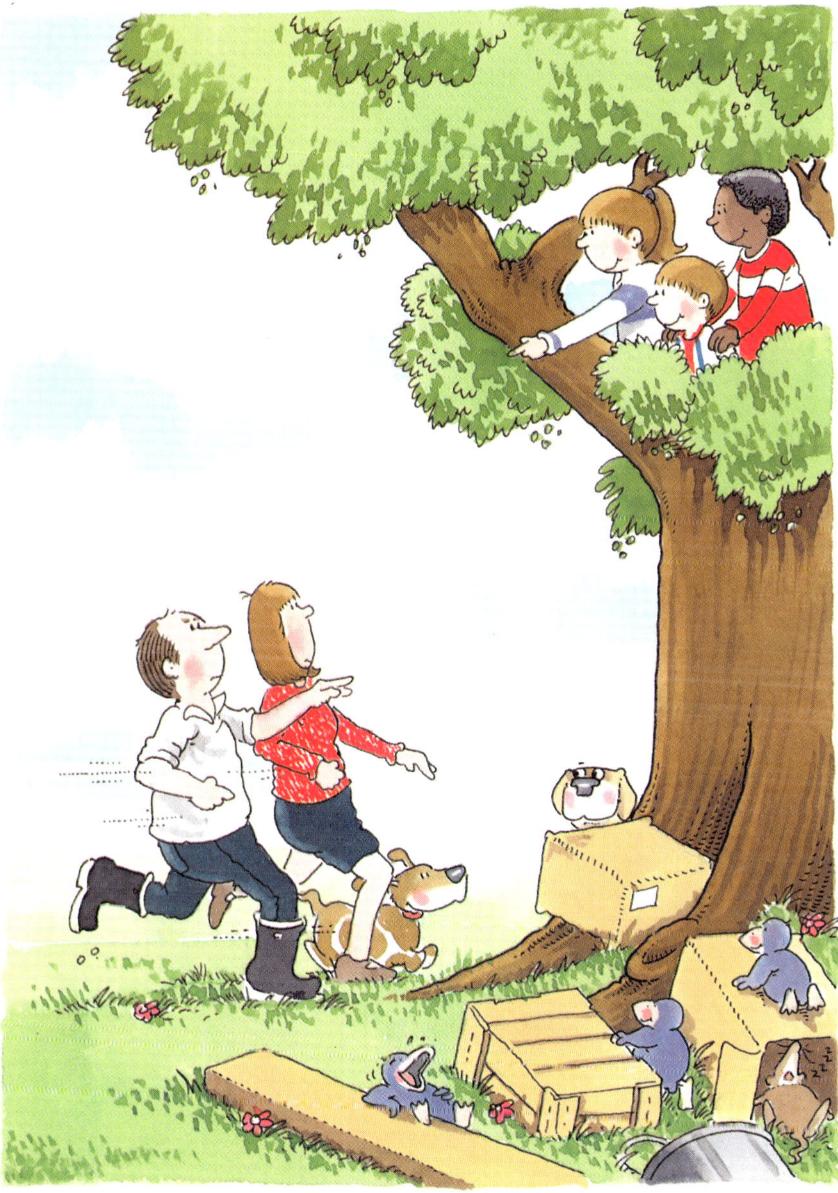

Dad and Mum

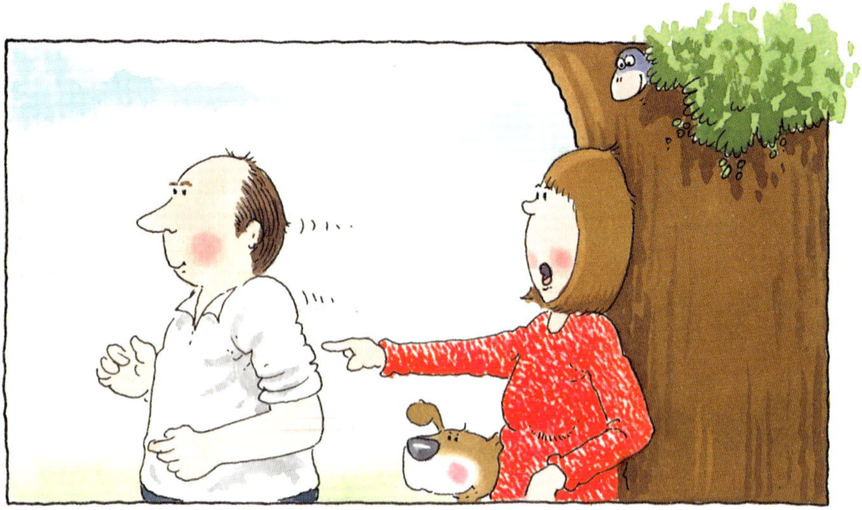

Dad and Mum help.

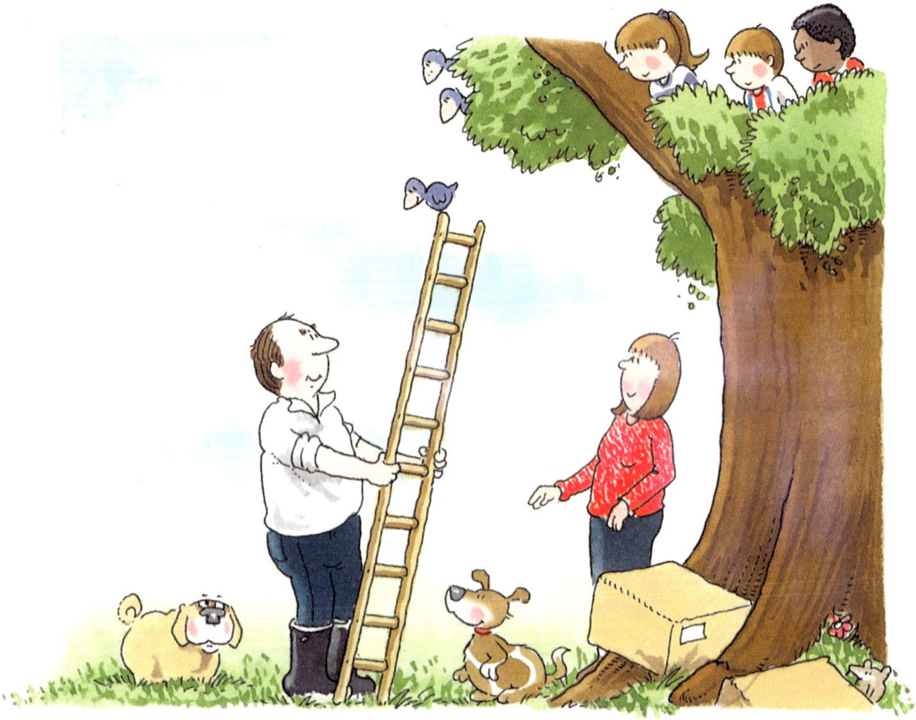

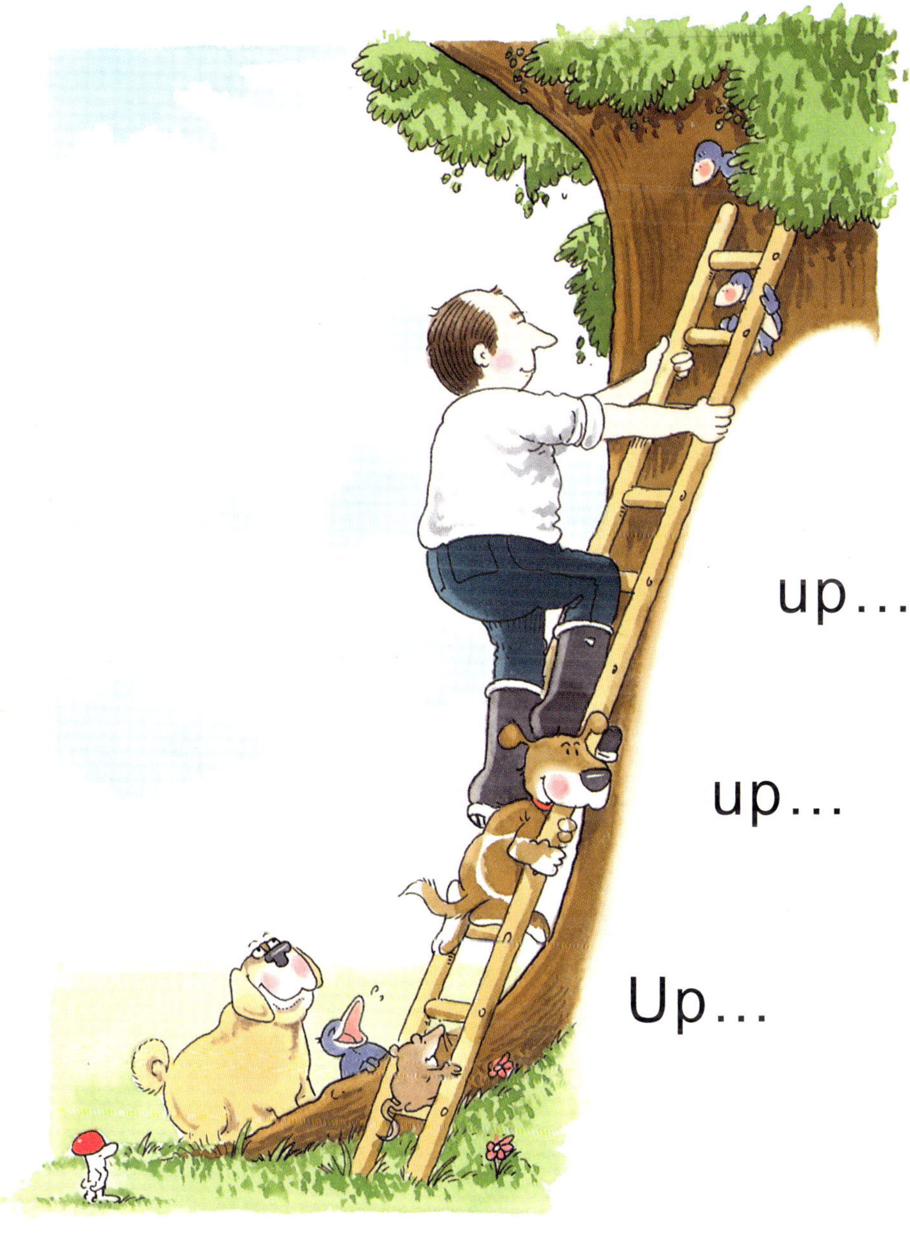

up...

up...

Up...

Dad went up.

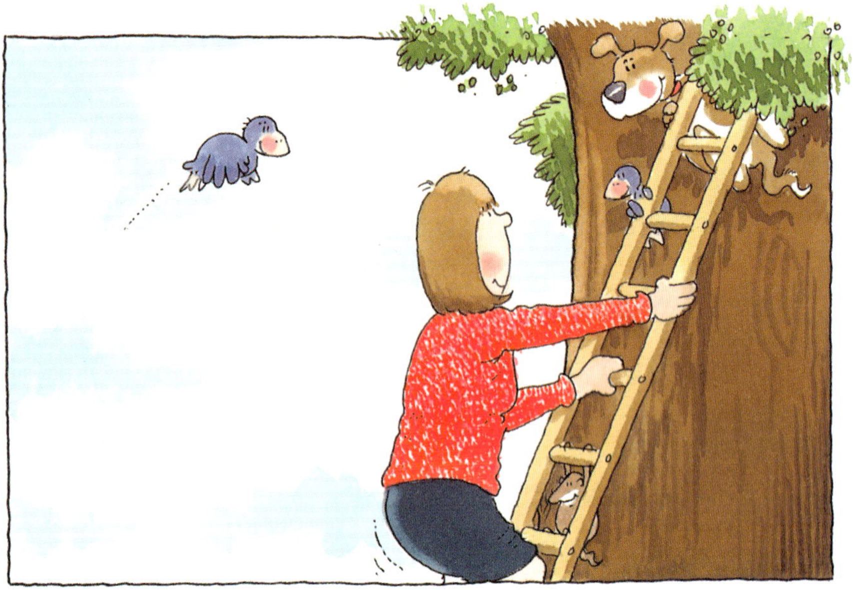

Up went Mum.

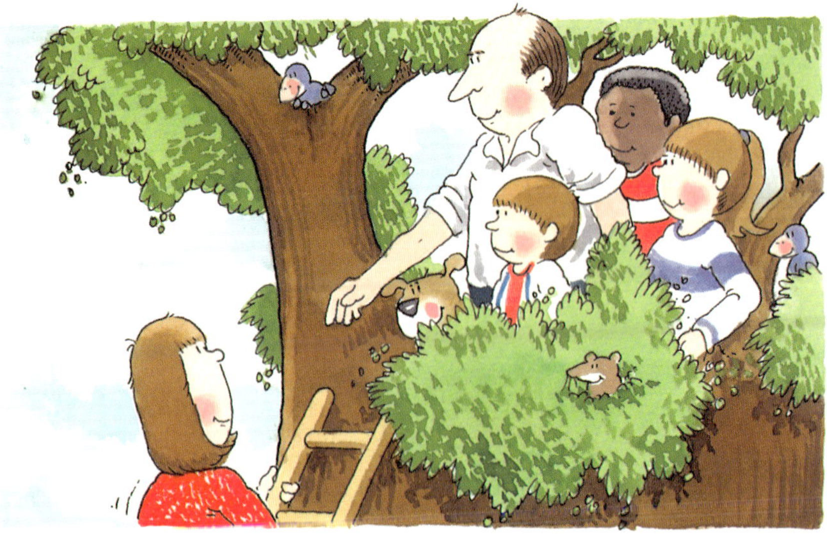

Mum went up to help.

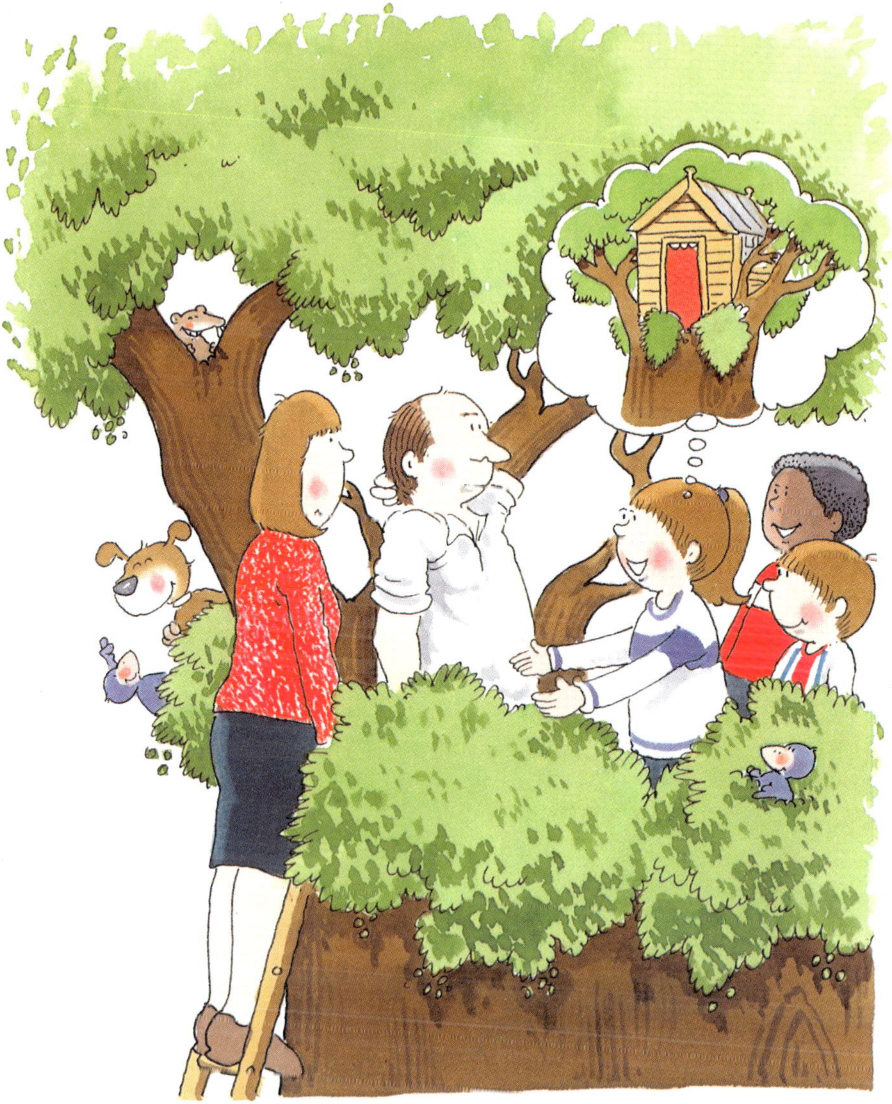

Mum and Dad
went up to help.

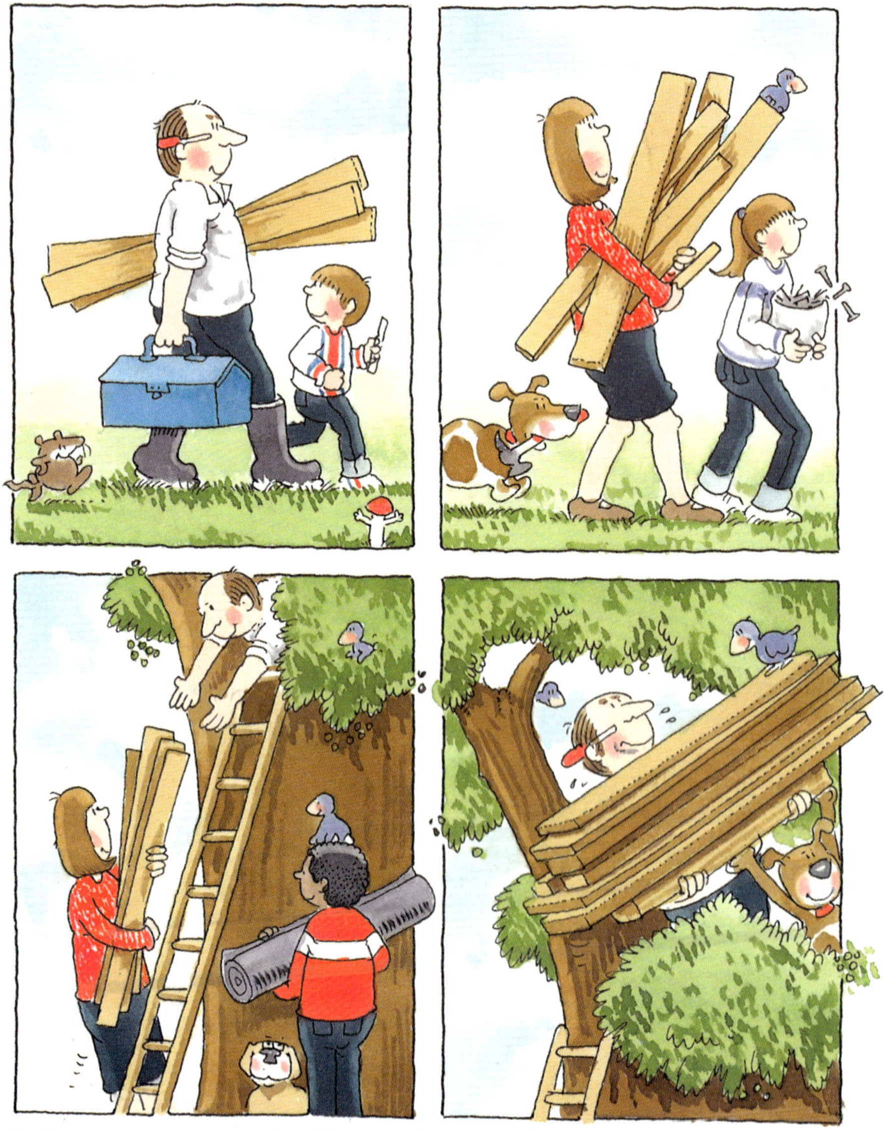

Mum and Dad help
Ben and Pen and Rob.

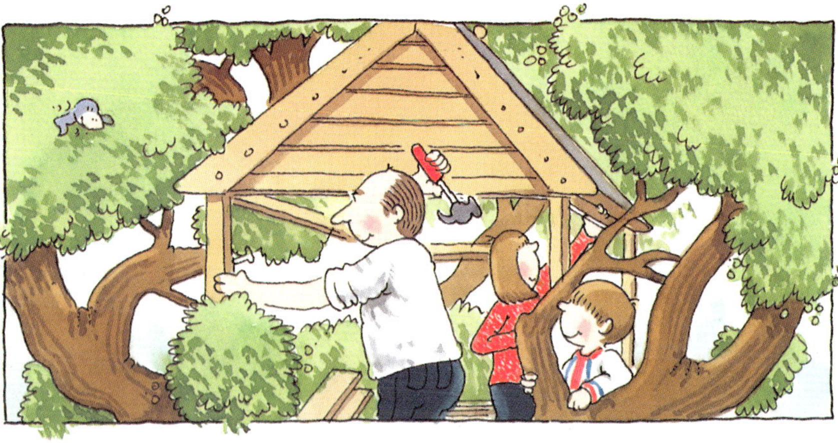

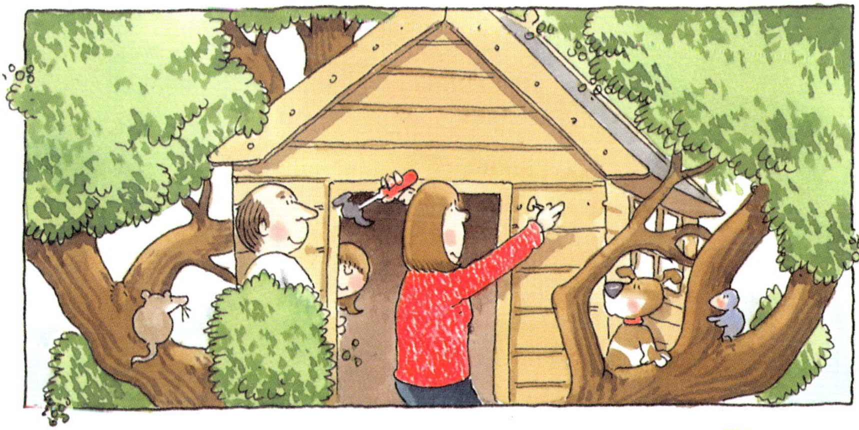

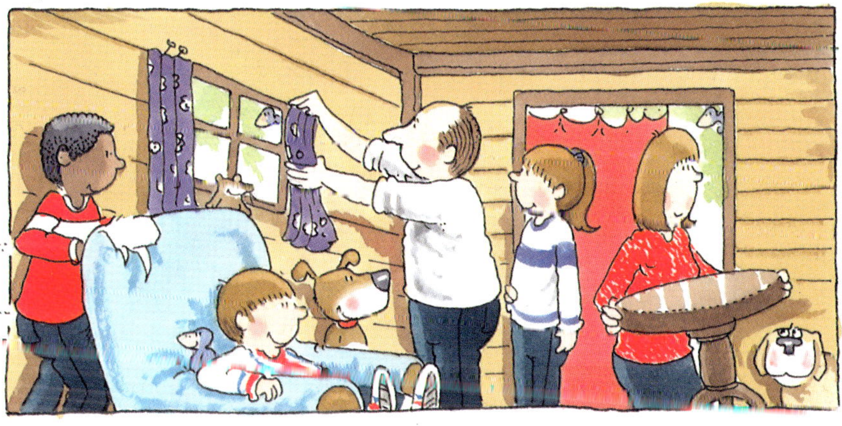

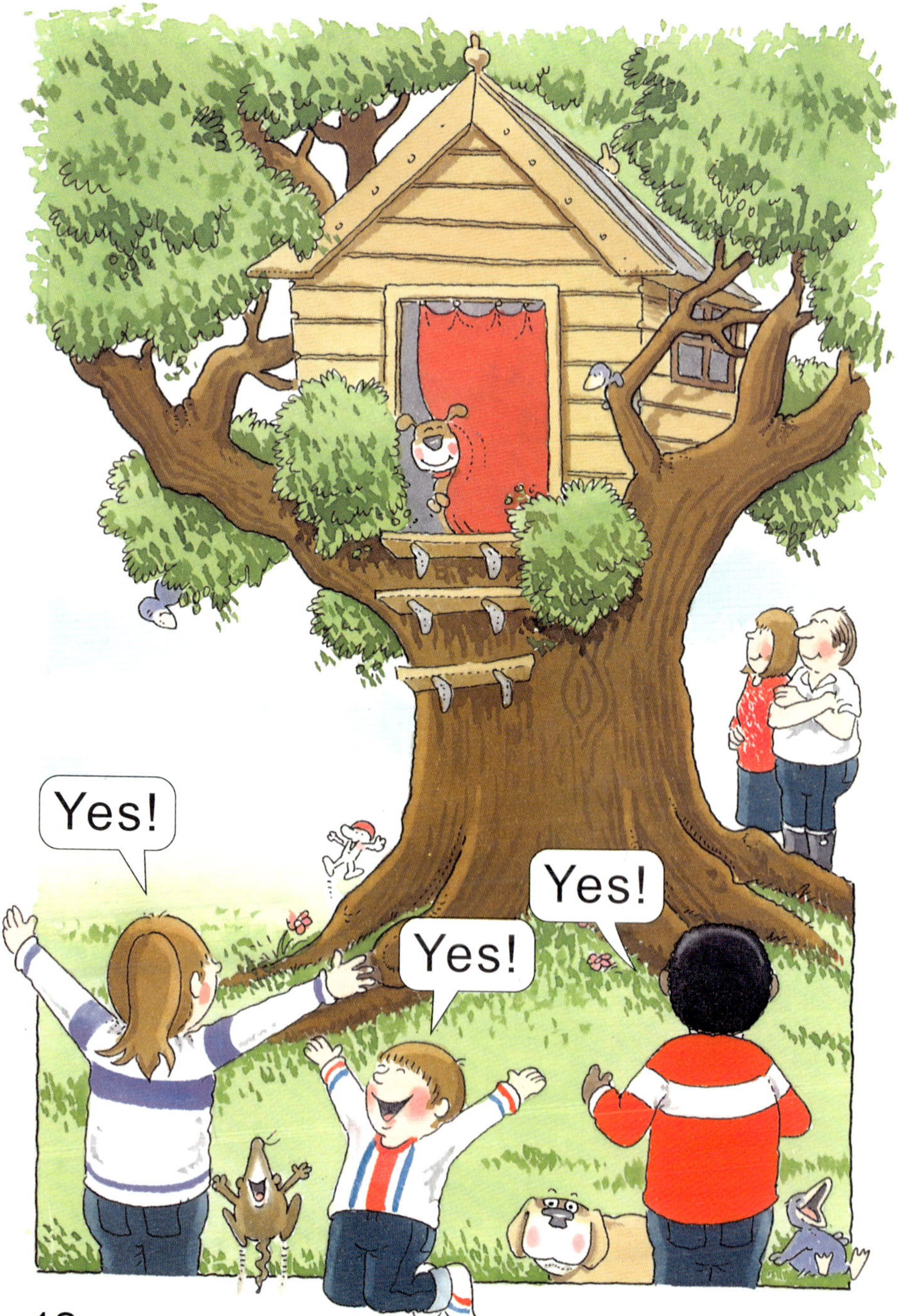
Yes!
Yes!
Yes!